The Strangest Sandwich In The World...
And Other Silly Stuff

A Collection of Poetry for Kids
By Rachel Sambrooks

Still Growing

About The Publisher

McKnight & Bishop are always on the lookout for great new authors and ideas for exciting new books. If you write or if you have an idea for a book, email us:

info@mcknightbishop.com

Some things we love are: undiscovered authors, open-source software, crowd-funding, Amazon/Kindle, social networking, faith, laughter and new ideas.

Visit us at: www.mcknightbishop.com

Copyright © 2015 by Rachel Sambrooks

The right of Rachel Sambrooks to be identified as the Author of the Work has been asserted by her in accordance with the Copyright, Designs and Patents Act 1988.

All rights reserved. No part of this publication may be reproduced, stored in a retrieval system, or transmitted, in any form or by any means without the prior written permission of the publisher, nor be otherwise circulated in any form of binding or cover other than that in which it is published and without a similar condition being imposed on the subsequent purchaser.

ISBN 978-1-905691-35-7

A CIP catalogue record for this book is available from the British Library

First published in 2015 **McKnight & Bishop Still Growing**, an imprint of:

>McKnight & Bishop Ltd.
>28 Griffiths Court, Bowburn, Co. Durham, DH6 5FD
>http://www.mcknightbishop.com
>info@mcknightbishop.com

This book has been typeset in **Champagne & Limousines** and Orange Juice.
Printed and bound in Great Britain by McKnight & Bishop Ltd, Durham

This book is dedicated to Isabella and Francesca
for the inspiration and the giggling at the funny bits.

TO THE READER:
Here's a collection of rhyme crimes and silly stuff, with strange sandwiches, mythic monsters, lost glue and all manner of weird and wonderful verses. If you giggle, make a squiggle and have a go yourself!

MY NAME IS

Contents

Hello 6

Funny Food 7

Affable Animals 10

Mythical Mirth And Monsters 15

A Very Silly Superhero 18

Ask A Silly Question 20

Silly School 23

Scared Silly! 26

Other Silly Silly Stuff 28

Enough Of The Silly Stuff 41

Hello..

Hello hello hello hello
Buongiorno, bonjour, how do you do?
Konnichiwa, Ola, Guten tag to you
Ahoy, a joy to meet you, Salam, Ni Hao
Bom dia, Shalom, Salute, Ciao,
Hello hello hello hello
Let's all bellow – HELLO!

Funny Food

Smelly Jelly

I made a lovely jelly it was orange
It was smelly

It wafted out the kitchen and out into the street
Everyone stopped and sniffed and shouted loud
'What is this wafting citrus cloud?
What is this tasty treat?
This wonderment
This culinary feat?'

And I declared,
'It is my smelly jelly!
I made it while I watched the telly
I have made it oh so sweet
Would you like a bit to eat?'

Everyone said yeah! Got onto their feet
And out into the street
Where we danced
and pranced

That's how my jelly
Made a party because it was
a
Yummy yummy, sniffy, orangey,
sweet and smelly jelly!

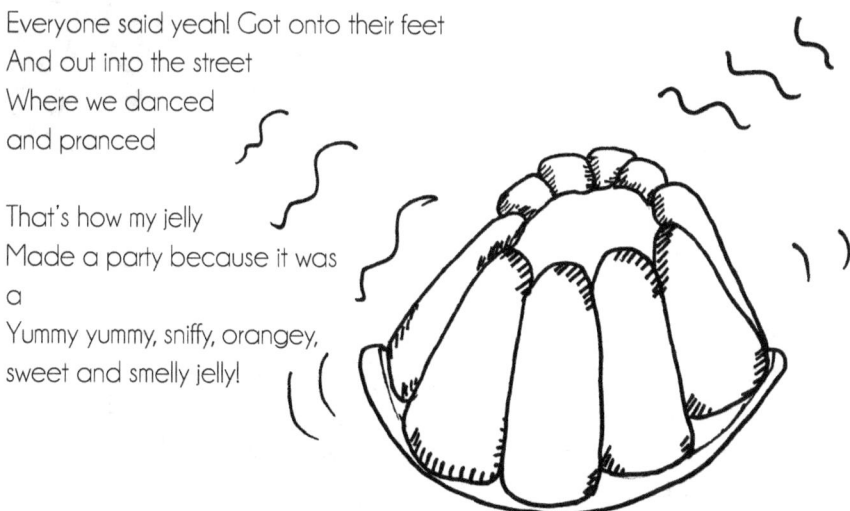

The Strangest Sandwich In The World...

For my lunch today
I won't eat school dinners
Whatever you say

I'm making the strangest sandwich in the
world you see
I'm going to eat it and you can't stop me

Some butter on bread
And then fish spread

Jam and ham, spam and yam
Cheese and peas and herbal teas
For added taste, a donkey's sneeze
Sauce, chocolate of course
Ice-cream that tastes supreme
Pickles and cake and spicy snake

I'm making the strangest sandwich in the world
you see
And I'm going to eat it you can't stop me

Lamb biryani and tofu,
Chicken tikka, onions, pitta
Pilau Rice, sugar mice and Irish stew
Garlic and burger to chew
Add a kebab
That'll taste fab
Blancmange and duck a l'orange
Chilli that's kickin', jerk chicken

Now to make it much much higher
I'm adding a tractor tyre

I'm making the strangest sandwich in the world you see
I'm going to eat it you can't stop me

Would you like to add some things
Make sure it really zings?

The washing up bowl
Plates and cheese grater
That'll save time later
Another slice of bread on top
And that's where I stop – or not…

On top of that – I'll eat my hat

It's the strangest sandwich in the world
And I made it!
Do you want to taste a little bit?
Or shall I eat it?

I have made the strangest sandwich
in the world
And it tastes disgusting. …

Anyone have a bucket I can borrow?
And do you know a funny thing?
I'm having hot dinners tomorrow

Affable Animals

Aardvark

Aardvark! You first animal in the dictionary
The only thing I know about you
Is that you like to be first in the queue
I imagine you are enormous and promontory

I expect you have a huge elephant trunk
Teeth that go clunk, a tiny mouse tail,
A massive mouth like a whale
And a hundred eyes like a fly

Aardvark I bet you eat buildings for breakfast
And feast on fleas for lunch, make them last
You don't have dinner, because you're an
Aardvark!!!

What's that when I look in the dictionary?
Page 1, word 1
AARDVARK
Oh. An aardvark is a medium sized animal.
BUT …
What if they are wrong
And an AARDVARK
Is hiding in the jungle
With an enormous and giant
Huge elephant trunk, teeth that go clunk
A tiny mouse tail and mouth like a whale
And a hundred eyes like a fly
That is MY
Aardvark

Flying Lizards

Have you ever seen a lizard in a blizzard?
A snake in the baking hot sun or
A dinosaur on the sea shore?
Unlikely as they prefer to hide in corners
And holiday underground when it's too cold or too hot
Especially dinosaurs.
They liked it so much they stayed there,
Tyrannosaurus never even saw us
That is why you see fossils underground and
Their footprints in the sand

Either that or a meteorite hit the earth
WHACK!
But I imagine they are on holiday
And coming back

My Pet Matt

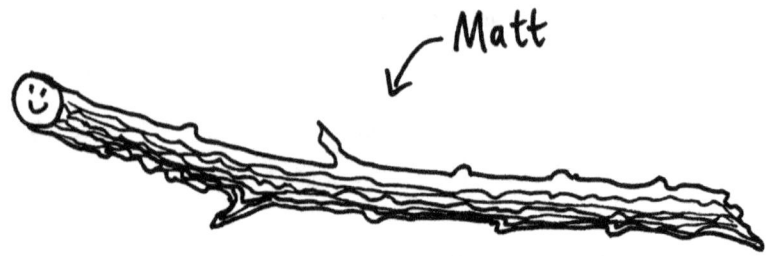

I found a puppy in the street this week
I took him home cos his life was bleak

He was brown and short and still and grey
But he was my best friend anyway

I called him Matt, well fancy that, a pet called Matt

When I got him home my mum said 'Unclean! What's that'
That's no puppy that's a rat!'

I lost Matt down the back of the sofas
Mum called Pest Control they're no loafers

Mum said 'Get rid of the rat!'
Was this the end of Matt?

'No' said Pest Control, 'Missus,
You're mad, you need glasses, your eyesight's bad'

'This is not a dog or a rat or a cat with a wig
This is in fact a small brown twig

And you called him Matt?'
Well fancy that a twig called Matt.'

Twig Matt went for a walk with me everyday
I taught him tricks like sit and stay
Then another dog came to play, they played all day

They went swimming by the river bank
Getting wetter and wetter
But he didn't come back, in fact he sank
I think Matt liked the park better

So now I got a new pet, his name is Mark
But Mum said he's just a piece of bark

Well fancy that, pet bark called Mark

Kittens and Fluffy Things

Fluffy fluffy kitty kitty jumping on the ground
Fluffy fluffy kitty kitty what is that you've found?
Fluffy fluffy kitty kitty pouncing on a rat
Fluffy fluffy kitty kitty curled up in my lap
Fluffy fluffy kitty kitty you are so so cute
Fluffy fluffy kitty kitty stop scratching me you brute
Fluffy fluffy kitty kitty with your tiny claws
Fluffy fluffy kitty kitty disobeys the laws

Mythical Mirth And Monsters

Unicorn

Unicorns are cooler than snakes
Unicorns have just one horn
And use them to mix cakes

Minotaurs have great big roars
Mermaids have great big claws
Pegasus is a horse that flies
But they do exist - as horseflies!

Little Ponies

My little pony isn't like all the others, she's no unicorn
She doesn't have a rainbow or wings or a horn.
She isn't pink and she doesn't eat cupcakes
She can't fly and she rarely has parties for all her mates
And her dashing isn't very rainbow- y and her prancing is the average amount
And her whinnying is glorious and she doesn't talk with a squeaky pout

I found her in a field, my little pony. She's brown and a Shetland.
She's chubby and likes carrots. My little pony is real, I know that's bland.
But she still likes birthday parties and she's my little pony.

Mother Dragon

Mother dragon lay curled around, her young sleeping for millennia
Keeping them warm on their bed of gold, soft fire tinging the air
Allowing none to pass

She is the guardian protector, only leaving to take to the skies
Master of the flight path, she watches over them
Allowing none to pass

And when they hatch she will be, all seeing undying watching over them
The guardian protector, her spikes run down her spine, across her iron clad coat
Allowing none to pass

She is majestic in her magnificence, but does all in service to her treasured young
The cave sleeps peacefully, but the volcano rages in her heart in case
Anyone tries to pass

And one day they will grow cracking out of stone shells, to live amongst us, some say
Ancient and wise and then she will let go of her dominating authority
Don't mess with mother dragon,
Don't go creeping into her cave to steal her gold
A power lies within her lizard heart, her fire breathing protection
Only her dragon young shall pass this way.
Mother of the skies,
Allows them to fly free, masters of their flight patterns
They shall pass.

I made up my own mythical monster, it's called a Snurkle....

I Wish I Was A Snurkle

I wish I was a Snurkle
I could Snurkle all day long
And float in my snurkly pool
Mess about like a snurkly fool

I wish I was a Snurkle
Snurkles are always happy
They don't worry about the weather
Their tails are usually flappy

I wish I was a Snurkle
Snurkles never have to work
They sing and dance all day
And on their faces is a snurkly smirk

I wish I was a Snurkle
Much better than a Blamblurk
Who gets bored at school all day
And always has to do their homework

I wish I was a Snurkle
Though of course I know
That Snurkles are a mystery to me
And they live somewhere over the sea

What do you think a Snurkle looks like?
Where does a Snurkle live?
What do Snurkles cook?
If you catch one, can I come and take a look?

A Very Silly Superhero

What would be your silly superpower? I would be invisible but only in the dark...

"If I had a Superpower," said the Snail

If I had a superpower said the snail
I would have two long trunks with roots that move
And stride around on them, run
Leap whole puddles in a single bound
Go from here to the bottom of the garden in less than two hours
Live in the beautiful, fresh, green green leaves
Of the cabbages

I would race pigeons and run from cats
I would save other snails from eating the wrong vegetables
I would create a land for snails full of cabbages
With my huge giant branches and the big old scoopers on the end
And I would be the Super Snail and everyone would look up at me
In the beautiful, fresh, green green leaves
Of the cabbages.

Really? Scoffed the other snails
They laughed and laughed and laughed
But Super Snail wanted a super power and so he laid in wait
Until Mr Gloucester started gardening late
And Super Snail slid up the huge trunks of his legs
And he slid down the branches of Mr Gloucester's arms and he
Slid down to the big old scooper hands at the end
He waved his tiny tentacle eye at Mr Gloucester. Who was scared of snails!

Mr Gloucester screamed 'ARGH!'
Mr Gloucester ran, jumping over a puddle
'Whheeeeee' shouted Super Snail
'SNAIL!' shouted Mr Gloucester
He ran all along the garden in less than two seconds
Super Snail leapt from his hand and landed in the cabbages
Mr Gloucester kept running out of the garden
Around and around and back into the house
Where he washed his hands and determined never to go out again.

The other snails followed the trail that Super Snail had left
And they all lived happily ever after
In the beautiful, fresh, green green leaves
Of the cabbages.

Ask A Silly Question........

Twenty Questions

Let's play 20 questions, answer the questions yes or no
Or something else, or maybe.
Is it my turn first?
Why do earwigs not wear wigs or have ears?
Are your toes the wrong way round?
Can you really touch the ground?
Are fairy sneezes like small warm breezes?
Do unicorns eat hula hoops off their horns?
Does Santa Claus get a round of applause?
If goats were kids and kids wore floats which swimming pool would have the most moats?
Did the Vikings live before my Nan and did a Viking have to be a man?
Do restaurants serve ants that rest?
Do hippopotami have a nest?
Does the Tooth Fairy resist the dentist?
Do Pirates shop at Arrrrrrrrgos?
Are cockatoos like cockathrees and are there cockafours that like to peck on doors?
Are tealights made of tea?
When you open a book do the words fall out? Do letters spill inside your head?
Where do the invisible worlds go when you wake up and the dreams flow down the drainpipe of memory?
When there's boring stuff on the telly how do I make a bottom burp that's really smelly, so all the others leave the room and I turnover and pretend it was a goat that took the remote?
Are you still there?

Yes or no? Or something else?
Or maybe? Now it's your go!....

What Do You Want To Be When You Grow Up?

When I grow up I want to be a hippo because they are cute but also scarier than polar bears who are proper scary and munch penguins for breakfast.
OR
When I grow up I want to be a skyscraper so people can pay huge money to eat in my rooftop restaurant
OR
When I grow up I'm going to live on the beach in a hut
and I won't get the bus to work but sell seashells on the seashore
like that famous seashell selling woman and
I will be a bore on the seashore
When you ask me about tide times I will know them all
and will fix my clock depending on if the water is lapping at my door
 or so far away I can't see it more than the tip of the top of my fingernail

I won't shop at ASDA I will order in fresh seaweed and mussels
and chips and mermaids will be my friend
and I will have a boat and make a dolphin my pet
but not keep him on a lead
but let him swim free in to the sea and call him Dave
because I bet there aren't many dolphins called Dave
(Even though it is a very popular human name).

You can chant along to this if you like...
Where's My Glue, I Have No clue?
(For the children of Hounslow Library)

Where's my glue, I have no clue?
Where's my glue, I have no clue?

I want to make a rocket and fly it to the moon
I want to make it out of card and boxes and a spoon
But I cannot find my gluestick, no, I cannot find my glue!

Where's my glue, I have no clue?
Where's my glue, I have no clue?

I've got a cardboard box full of supermarket tins
I wrestled from a fox to take it from the bins
It needs to stick together with glitter on it too
But I cannot find my gluestick, no, I cannot find my glue!

Where's my glue, I have no clue?
Where's my glue, I have no clue?

I looked under the bed, I looked under the stairs
I looked under my head, I looked the chairs
But I cannot find my gluestick, no, I cannot find my glue

Have I looked inside my pocket? It's my glue!
I can make this rocket
Now all I need to do, to make this rocket, shine and spin
Is to finish it off with some colouring in

I've got the red, I've got the green, I've got the purple too
But I cannot find my blue pen, no, I cannot find my blue
Where's my BLUE, I have no clue?
But green will do

Silly School

What if your teacher, wasn't JUST a teacher?....

My Teacher

My teacher says she's just a teacher
But I noticed her mythical creature
lying underneath her desk
there's a dragon's nest

My teacher says
she's just a teacher
But she's got a
magic broom
Hidden in her bedroom
And in her kitchen live a
cat and a frog
And next to that lies a magic dog

My teacher says she's just a teacher
But she's got a magic wand
Which she hides in her garden pond
She just won't say
But I know she's got a book with a spell
For every day

My teacher says she's just a teacher
But I noticed her distinctive feature
She wears a witch's hat
And that is that

Homework Excuses

My dog ate my homework, he thought it was a bone
But first a crocodile ate my homework he was on his way home
And as he was walking to the zoo, he saw my homework which
Had been picked up by a pigeon, from my bag, unzipped in a glitch

So a pigeon stole my homework and flew off with it to Naples
Then a crocodile ate it, but couldn't swallow the staples
so he left it there for a bit, then I send my dog to look for it
But when he found it he ate it too
That's why it's not in front of you

But no worries it came out the other end ok
I'll wash it and dry it and piece it together
And let you have it Wednesday

Reading

Reading a book that's taken me in
I'm inside the book and I'm not
getting out again
My nose is in the book and
everyone's
Shouting at me but I can't hear them
I'm walking down the road
With my nose in the book and

I step in a puddle and into a creek
I'm washed away floating on my back
But I don't notice cos my nose is in the book
And I'm not racing down a river
But miles away
With wizards and wands and magic school
With dragons and unicorns and leaping horses
With dogs and evil people

And as I float down the river, I'm washed out to sea
So far across the ocean, no-one on shore can see me
But I don't notice it myself
Because my nose is in the book and I'm not there
I'm flying over mountains with an elf
I'm hiding in a forest and dancing with a bear

The sea waves rise and the water splashes in my face,
But my nose is in the book and I'm not there
The tide takes me to a desert island, I reach the last page
As I take it away the sun warms my face
The sand dries on my back and I wipe away a tear

I shut the book and look around at the desert island, lush and green
Under a bush, another book I find, and started reading, unseen.

Scared Silly!

We can all get scared about silly things, but remember that shadowy pointy thing in the corner is just a coathanger, or a scarf or something really really not a monster under the bed...

Monsters Under The Bed

What's that thing on the floor
Next to the door
It looks like a....
No way it can't be a....
Spider with no legs
Cockroach curled up
Beetle balled
A wingless moth

It's by my foot!
Must pick it up and take a look
But what if it's a ....
Flea
A flightless fly
A bug
I kick it on the rug

Why isn't that amazin'
It's just a dried up raisin

Night - Mare

At night the nightmare races across the darkened skies
The horse that makes grown ups tremble and quake
The horse whose eyes glow red in the dark

At night the nightmare races across the cloudless sleeps
And into our dreams, she races jumps and leaps
At night the nightmare rules her kind all follow in her wake
The fear she brings with her makes grown ups shiver and shake

I wait and wait to see her, I wonder who she is
The night-mare galloping through dreams for thrills
Breathing hot air onto the window, she whinnies
Clip clopping at the sills

At night the nightmare wanders into thoughts and
In the web above my bed, my dreamcatcher whisks her away
The nightmare has to end.

Other Silly Silly Stuff

I Love Bubbles I Do.

Bubbles in puddles
Bubbles blown
Bubbles in foam
Bubble on the phone
Bubbles in the kitchen
Bubbles up the stairs
Bubbles on a chicken
Bubbles in my hairs
Bubbles bubbles bubbles

Bubbles floating through the air
I love them all up there
I love making bubbles in the bath with soapy foam
It's the works, they're bottom burps!
I love Bu Bu Bu BBBBBBLLLLLEEEESSSSS

In The Car......

In the back of the car,
That's where we are, in the back of the car

I get car sick, in the back of the car
I kick my sis, in the back of the car

Some kids have TVs, in the back of the car
I just count trees, in the back of the car

One two threes, in the back of the car
I try to play I spy, in the back of the car

Just me and my little eye, in the back of the car
No one knows where we are, in the back of the car

We're going really far, in the back of the car
Are we nearly there yet? In the back of the car

I'm going to sleep, in the back of the car
Kicking my feet, in the back of the car
Eating some sweets, in the back of the car

What? We've arrived and I'm out of the car
That's really great ,cos I really hate, the back of the car

Magical Mystery Tour Guide To Childhood

Whoop whoop ding dong all aboard
The magical mystery tour through childhood
Here we stop at first you're teeny tiny baby
Poop and eat, poop and eat
Blarp there goes another one
Ickle wickle baby burps
Ickle wickle baby snoozes in a cot
Ickle wickle baby wakes up crying in the night
Ickle wickle… right that's enough back on the bus

Beep beep whoop whoop ding ding all aboard
The magical mystery tour through childhood

Here you are age 2
A toddler through and through
You run over there you run over there
And when you stop who knows who cares
Your mum does when you run in the car park
STOP toddler STOP!
And eat your food don't mash it on your face
You dropped it on the floor and laugh and laugh
Toddler toddler not for much longer…
Right that's enough back on the bus

Bing bing, beep beep whoop whoop ding ding all aboard
The magical mystery tour through childhood

Right here you are age 5
What's that big house there? Why am I dressed in these boring clothes? What's going on? Whose that big lady? She's not my mum she's my teacher.
Argh I'm in school, I wondered when that would feature.

Maths and English, take your turn, so much to learn
Right that's enough, back on the bus

Plop plop bing bing beep beep whoop whoop ding ding all aboard
The magical mystery tour through childhood

Bang bang booosh....
Oops the bus seems to have broken down
We've stopped here aged 10. That was quick!
Let's stop rushing that'll do the trick and walk it from here
Without a frown

Scream Time Screen Time

It used to be I scream you scream we all scream for ice cream
But now it's I scream, you scream, we all scream for screen!
It's screen time!

Screen time one hour no more, go away, shut the door
Screen time ten minutes left, go away, shut the door
Screen time five minutes left, that's that, open the door

No No No! You scream
You scream, we scream, we all scream
For more screen time

Service Stations

The most exciting place in the world
The service station
Burgers and chicken never tasted so good
The toilets are full of travellers from exotic other towns
At different ends of the motorways

Shop is full of toys you'll never buy
Because no-one will buy you a pillow for £10 that looks like a rabbit
No, no, no! Nor a travel mug that is also a torch.

We sit in a café whilst we wait and eat
A blueberry muffin whilst everyone groans at the prices.
So we watch all the travellers from exotic other towns
At different ends of the motorway.

Havens

Inspired by 'Little Houses' by Angela Topping

Two chairs, a draped sheet, a broom
My garden house, outside but in
By myself, warm and cosy
A glow not seen by anyone else

Reading books under cover of kitchen table
A world away, imagination in flight
Blanket shields the exits
A torch lights up the words

In woods with fallen branches, I drag and build
All leaves and twigs and pretend to see
Fairies, elves, invisible, wandering free
Floating dandelion clocks, in sunbeams

In havens built from mud pies, twigs and trees
In havens built from duvet covers, pillows, brooms
In havens built from chairs and sheet, never quite complete
You sit undiscovered, but find yourself

My Nan's Bigger Than Your Nan

My nan's bigger than your nan
Don't you know it's true
She could tear down walls and chomp your nan in two

No! My nan's bigger than your nan
She's got knitting needles and fighting beetles

My nan's better than your nan
Her cakes are exquisite it's true

My nan's better than your nan
She does great cuddles too

My nan's better than your nan
She's invited you for tea

But my nan's better than your nan
She's invited your nan too, that's three

My nan's said thanks, we'd love to.

BORED

I'M SO BORED
Bored bored bored
Don't tell me to do the housework and tidy up my room
I've finished all my jobs and the battery on my games are doomed
So I AM BORED!
I don't know what to do
SO BORED
I'm drawing on the carpet
SO BORED
I rub it off cos I'll mark it
SO BORED
I'm lying on my bed
SO BORED
Standing on my head
SO BORED
I tell someone else I'm
SO BORED
I tell them over and over
SO BORED
They ignore me until I go away
SO BORED
I go outside to play
SO BORED
There's nothing there to do
SO BORED
I try kicking a ball or two
SO BORED
If only I had an idea
SO BORED

Perhaps
SO
I
Bored
Could
Bored
Write
Bored
A
Bored
Poem
About how
Bored
I am
So I did.
And I'm NOT bored anymore!

Advice For Time Travellers

If you're going to go backwards in time
Please be careful of the dinosaurs, they fight
And are known to bite
And if you end up in the Dark Ages
Be careful you don't knock into Knights and Pages
It is very dark
And if you travel to World War 2 watch out for bombs too
It's no lark

And if you go into the future, with time inflation
Please send me a message in a time travelling bottle
With the lottery numbers and the latest Playstation

To The Young Poet....

You don't have to be a wizard
To write a magic poem
Think of a word that rhymes like lizard
And write it down
Like crown
And frown
Or gate and late

And you know it's not a crime
If they don't really rhyme
Like frog and rabbit
Just think some words, imagine more
Who knows what secrets lie
behind your poetry door?

I Am.....

I am braver than a butterfly
I am cooler than the sky
I am taller than the green green sea
I am sweeter than the broccoli
I am richer than a mouse
I am braver than a house
I am nicer than a chair
I am fresher than a bear!

Well that was a very silly poem, I bet you could do better.
What are you?
Write your own!

I am ....

I am ....

I am ....

I am ....

I am ....

I am ....

Enough Of The Silly Stuff...

It's time to go

Goodbye

Goodbye it's not forever
Goodbye I won't say never
Goodbye I'll see you again
Goodbye I'll miss you and then
I won't say goodbye I'll stay with you here
And never leave you in it.....
Ok, I'll be back in a minute
I won't say goodbye I'll try
To write a letter or an email I'll send
With big hugs.
The end.

Acknowledgements

Thanks so much to those that have helped me this year, especially to Pete who is amazing and is the reason I can do all this writing lark. Thanks to Maria, Nicky and all at Apples and Snakes. Thanks to all the children at the SPINE Festival 2015 at Hounslow Library, Ann and Anita you were so helpful. Arts Network Sutton and Sutton Theatres thanks for encouraging the show, thank you!

Your Poems...

www.ingramcontent.com/pod-product-compliance
Lightning Source LLC
LaVergne TN
LVHW021741060526
838200LV00052B/3401